Take a trip to
ROMANIA

Keith Lye

Franklin Watts
London   New York   Sydney   Toronto

Facts about Romania

Area:
237,500 sq. km
(91,699 sq. miles)

Population:
22,830,000

Capital:
Bucharest

Largest cities:
Bucharest (1,961,000)
Braşov (335,000)
Constanţa (319,000)
Iaşi (310,000)
Timişoara (309,000)
Cluj-Napoca (300,000)

Official language:
Romanian

Religion:
Christianity

Main exports:
Machinery and equipment; fuels, minerals and metals; other manufactures; farm and forest products

Currency:
Leu

Franklin Watts
12a Golden Square
London W1

Franklin Watts Inc.
387 Park Avenue South
New York, N.Y. 10016

ISBN: UK Edition 0 86313 644 3
ISBN: US Edition 0 531 10468 0
Library of Congress Catalog Card No: 87-51069

Typeset by Ace Filmsetting Ltd.,
Frome, Somerset
Printed in Hong Kong

© Franklin Watts Limited 1988

Maps: Simon Roulstone
Design: Edward Kinsey
Stamps: Harry Allen International Philatelic Distributors
Photographs: Guy Arnold, 3, 5; Barnaby's Picture Library, 20; Tony Morrison, 17, 19, 26; Romanian Tourist Office, 7, 8, 14, 16, 21, 29, 30; Tony Stone Associates, 28; Zefa, 4, 6, 11, 12, 13, 15, 18, 22, 23, 24, 25, 27, 31
Front Cover: Zefa
Back Cover: Barnaby's Picture Library

The Socialist Republic of Romania is a country in southeastern Europe. It borders the Black Sea. The Danube, Europe's second longest river after the Volga, forms much of the southern border with Bulgaria. Romania also borders the USSR (Russia), Hungary and Yugoslavia.

3

Romania contains six main regions. The southern region, drained by the Danube and its many tributaries, is low-lying. It is called Walachia and has much fertile farmland. The capital, Bucharest, is located there.

A second region is Dobruja, a flat and marshy plain near the Black Sea. This region is rich in wildlife, including about 300 species of birds and many kinds of fish. Dobruja includes the Danube delta.

Transylvania, north of Walachia, contains most of Romania's mountains, including the Transylvanian Alps (or southern Carpathians), the Transylvanian plateau and plains in the northwest.

Moldavia, the fourth region, is in the northeast. It is famed for its painted churches. The painted monastery of Moldoviţa, in this picture, is in the fifth region of Bucovina, which lies northwest of Moldavia. Romania's sixth region is Banat in the southwest.

The picture shows some money and stamps used in Romania. The main unit of currency is the leu, which is divided into 100 banis.

WORLD MAP

Histria, on the coast about 50 km (30 miles) north of Constanţa, was founded by the Greeks in 657 BC. After the Romans conquered Romania in AD 106, it became a Roman town. The Romanian language, unlike other East European languages, is based on Latin.

In the Middle Ages, the country was divided into areas ruled by princes. The rulers lived in fortified castles. Bran Castle, near Braşov is linked with Vlad Ţepeş, the supposed model for Count Dracula.

Bucharest is Romania's capital and largest city. It has many beautiful buildings, including the Romanian Athenaeum, a 19th-century concert hall. It also contains many parks, lakes and woods.

New government buildings lie near the Stavropoleos Church (1724) in Bucharest. Romania has been ruled by the Communist party since 1947, when the last monarch, King Michael, gave up his throne.

Braşov, Romania's second largest city, is surrounded by mountains and winter resorts. Braşov's Town Hall in the picture contains a History Museum. Just over half of all Romanians live in cities and towns.

Constanţa, the country's third city and chief port, was founded by the Greeks in the 6th century BC. It has a fine National History and Archaeological Museum. Constanţa is now a major industrial city.

Cluj-Napoca is the capital of Transylvania. It is a major educational and industrial city, with the country's largest Roman Catholic cathedral. Most Romanians are Christians, although Communists are opposed to religious worship.

In 1985, about 16 million people were members of the Romanian Orthodox Church. There were also 1.2 million Roman Catholics and 30,000 Jews. The church in the picture is in the Dobruja region.

Romania has changed greatly in recent years. In 1950, farming employed 75 per cent of workers, as compared with 29 per cent today. But farming remains an important activity. Farmland covers 63 per cent of the land. The leading crops are maize (corn) and wheat.

The Danube delta contains some fertile farmland. Most of Romania's farmland is divided into collective farms, where farmers work together and share the profits, or state farms, where workers are paid wages.

Livestock farming is also important. Romania has more than 18 million sheep, 7 million cattle and about 15 million pigs. More and more farms now use modern machinery. Farm production is rising, while the number of farm workers is falling.

Romania is the second leading oil producer in eastern Europe after the USSR. But experts expect that the oil will run out in the mid-1990s. Romania's hydroelectric stations will then become more important in generating electricity.

Industry employs 38 per cent of Romanian workers. Besides oil, the country has coal and various metals. Many factories, such as this chemical works, have been built since 1947. The government owns all industries.

Romania exports manufactured goods including petroleum products and industrial equipment. Manufactures for home use are carefully checked by examiners, who ensure that they are of good quality.

23

Children between 6 and 16 get free education, including eight years at a primary school and two years at a secondary school. Most people speak Romanian. But there are also about 1.77 million Hungarians, 360,000 Germans and 1 million Gypsies in the country.

Most Romanians are proud of their ancient customs, including their regional costumes. However, in the cities, most people now wear typical western clothes. The man in the picture is wearing the traditional clothes associated with the northern Bucovina region.

Living standards in Romania are lower than in most of Europe. Food shortages often occur and only a few families have cars or television sets. These farm workers live in the Danube delta region.

The picture shows goulash (a spicy stew) being prepared for the many guests at a village wedding. Other popular foods include mamaliga, a corn (maize) mush, mititei (skinless sausages), cheeses and cakes.

Grilled meats are popular, while beef, chicken and pork are often stuffed with mixtures of such things as bacon, cheese, herbs and vegetables. Fish dishes include herring and sturgeon. Many people drink wine with meals, as in this restaurant in Braşov.

Folk music and dancing are ancient art forms. They are performed on holidays and at special occasions, such as weddings. The dancers in this picture come from Walachia. Romania's best known composer, Georges Enesco (1881–1955), used folk melodies in his work.

Many Romanians enjoy visits to the mountains. Many take part in winter sports, especially skiing. In summer, mountain climbing and hiking are popular activities. Soccer is the leading spectator sport.

Summer resorts with beautiful sandy beaches, such as Mamaia north of Constanța, line the Black Sea coast. The number of foreign tourists has increased from 100,000 in 1960 to 8 million in 1981.

Index

Arts 29

Banat 7
Bran Castle 11
Braşov 14, 28
Bucharest 12–13
Bucovina 7, 25

Carpathian Mountains 6
Chemical works 22
Clothes 25
Cluj-Napoca 16
Communist party 13, 16
Constanţa 15
Crops 18

Dancing 29
Danube River 3, 5, 19, 26
Dobruja 4, 17, 19, 26
Dracula, Count 11

Education 24
Enesco, Georges 29

Farming 18–20
Food 27–28

Government 13

History 10–11, 13
Histria 10
Hydroelectricity 21

Industry 21–23

Languages 10, 24
Living standards 26

Mamaia 31
Minorities 24
Moldavia 7
Moldoviţa 7
Money 8
Music 29

Oil production 21

Religion 16–17

Sheep 20
Sports 30
Stamps 8

Tourism 31
Transylvania 6, 16

JAN 2 5 1989

J949.8

BUCKHEAD BRANCH

Lye, Keith.
   Take a trip to Romania / Keith Lye.
-- New York : F. Watts, c1988.
   32 p. : col. ill. ; 22 cm.
   Includes index.
   Summary: A brief introduction, in text and photographs, to the geography, history, economy, culture, and people of Romania.
   ISBN 0-531-10468-0

R00532 74991

BHB

   1. Romania--Juvenile literature. I. Title

GA   08 DEC 88   17730387   GAPApc   87-51069